J
595.7
Por
Porter
The insect world

R398915
10.00

DATE DUE			
AG 21 '87			
NO 6 '87			
OC 10 '89			
DE 26 '89			
MY 22 '90			

GREAT RIVER REGIONAL LIBRARY
St. Cloud, Minnesota 56301

THE ANIMAL KINGDOM
THE INSECT WORLD
KEITH PORTER

Editorial planning
Jollands Editions

SCHOOLHOUSE PRESS, Inc.

Copyright © 1986 by Schoolhouse Press, Inc.
191 Spring Street, Lexington,
Massachusetts 02173-8087
ISBN 0-8086-1001-5

Original copyright, © Macmillan Education Limited 1986
© BLA Publishing Limited 1986

All rights reserved. No reproduction, copy or transmission of this publication may be made without written permission.

No paragraph of this publication may be reproduced, copied or transmitted without written permission of the publisher.

Designed and produced by BLA Publishing Limited,
Swan Court, East Grinstead, Sussex, England.

Also in LONDON · HONG KONG · TAIPEI · SINGAPORE · NEW YORK

A Ling Kee Company

Illustrations by Steve Lings/Linden Artists, Fiona Fordyce and BLA Publishing Limited
Colour origination by Chris Willcock Reproductions
Printed in Italy by G. Canale & C. S.p.A. — Torino

85/86/87/88   6 5 4 3 2 1

Acknowledgements
The Publishers wish to thank the following organizations for their invaluable assistance in the preparation of this book.

Rentokil
Shell

Photographic credits
t = top   b = bottom   l = left   r = right

cover: Anthony Bannister/NHPA

4 ZEFA; 5t Stephen Dalton/NHPA; 5b, 7 Aquila; 9 Reproduced by permission of the Director, British Geological Survey (NERC); 11t Stephen Dalton/NHPA; 11b, 12 Aquila; 13t A Shell photograph; 13b Biophoto Associates/NHPA; 15t, 15b Stephen Dalton/NHPA; 16 Biophoto Associates/NHPA; 17 Anthony Bannister/NHPA; 18 Biophoto Associates/NHPA; 19 Keith Porter; 21t A Shell photograph; 21b Stephen Dalton/NHPA; 22 Anthony Bannister/NHPA; 23 A Shell photograph; 24 Ivan Polunin/NHPA; 25 Anthony Bannister/NHPA; 26, 27t Stephen Dalton/NHPA; 27b, 28/29 Aquila; 29b James Carmichael/NHPA; 30 Anthony Bannister/NHPA; 31 ZEFA; 32 Keith Porter; 33 G.J. Cambridge/NHPA; 34, 35t Anthony Bannister/NHPA; 35b Stephen Dalton/NHPA; 37 Anthony Bannister/NHPA; 38 Ivan Polunin/NHPA; 39 Aquila; 40b Stephen Dalton/NHPA; 40/41, 41b Rentokil; 42t Aquila; 42b A Shell photograph; 43 Anthony Bannister/NHPA; 44 Aquila; 45t Stephen Dalton/NHPA; 45b NHPA

Note to the reader
In this book there are some words in the text which are printed in **bold** type. This shows that the word is listed in the glossary on page 46. The glossary gives a brief explanation of words which may be new to you.

Contents

Introduction	4	Butterflies and Moths	28
What is an Insect?	6	Crickets and Their Relatives	30
Before the Dinosaurs	8	One Pair of Wings	32
Thousands of Types	10	True Bugs and Beetles	34
Insect Skeletons	12	Water Insects	36
How Insects Move	14	Unusual Insects	38
Seeing and Feeling	16	Insects in Our Homes	40
Breathing and Feeding	18	Insects that Cause Harm	42
A Life Cycle	20	How Insects Help Us	44
Insects Everywhere	22		
Insect Builders	24	Glossary	46
Bees and Wasps	26	Index	48

Introduction

How much do you know about insects? Most of us only notice large insects and those that bite or sting. The rest we ignore as small, black creepy-crawling insects. In fact, the insect world is full of surprises.

Like all animals, each insect does a job. Without them our world would be very different.

A Tiny World

Insects live in a strange world. A slight breeze can blow them away. Grass blades become tree trunks. Pebbles are like mountains. Even raindrops turn into deadly pools.

On a summer day the ground can be very hot. At times, in the morning a thin layer of frost covers the same ground. We do not see or feel these things. We stand well above the world of the insect. Our warm bodies protect us from the cold. The body of an insect does not stay warm like ours. It cools down during the night.

Shapes for Life

Insects cope with their world in many ways. Millions of years of living has shaped each type of insect. Some are long and thin and live in tunnels. Others are shaped for flying.

No two types live in exactly the same place. Some insects survive where no others can. Young **midges** live in hot springs. They can stand temperatures that would fry other animals. One kind of fly even breeds in pools of oil.

▼ You can find insects almost anywhere on earth. Young midges live at temperatures up to 104°F in these hot springs at Yellowstone Park, Wyoming.

Introduction

Most insects live on or near plants. They are shaped and colored to look like parts of plants. Life is a constant battle for them. There are so many other animals who want to eat them.

Insect Skills

Insects make good use of their tiny world. Every insect has its own special skills. They use their feet and mouths as tools. Some have mouths which chisel into wood. Others use their jaws as tiny scissors.

Insects called **termites** live in huge nests. Each type of termite has a different shape and skill. They have soldiers, nurses, food gatherers, and queens. The soldiers have huge jaws, and the queens have fat bodies full of eggs.

Many insects make their own building materials. Some use silk to make their homes. Bees use wax to make perfectly shaped nests. Even humans make use of some insect skills. Silk thread and wax for candles both come from insects.

▲ Honeybees are expert builders. These food storage houses would put many human builders to shame.

▼ Leaf cutter ants cut and gather leaves. They eat a fungus that grows on the leaves.

What is an Insect?

All large animals, such as fish, birds, and humans, have a bony **skeleton** and a soft skin. This helps to form the shape of the animal. The bodies of insects are different. They have a hard skin called an **exoskeleton**. It protects and shapes the insect.

The insect's skin stops its body from drying out. There are other small animals that have exoskeletons. Unlike insects, some of them dry out quickly. One is the woodlouse. It has to live in a damp place. If it did not, it would die.

Animals in Groups

All animals belong to groups. Insects belong to the biggest group, called the **arthropods**. Arthropod is a Greek word which means "jointed-feet." All insects have legs which are like small pieces of tubing stuck together. The legs can bend where the tubes join.

Insects are the only arthropods to have six legs. Others in the group have eight legs and often many more. The spiders, with eight legs, are most like the insects. Most insects also have wings.

All insects have a body made up of three main parts. These are the head, a **thorax** which is in the middle, and a "tail" or **abdomen**.

▼ The arthropod group is split into four sections. One section includes all the insects.

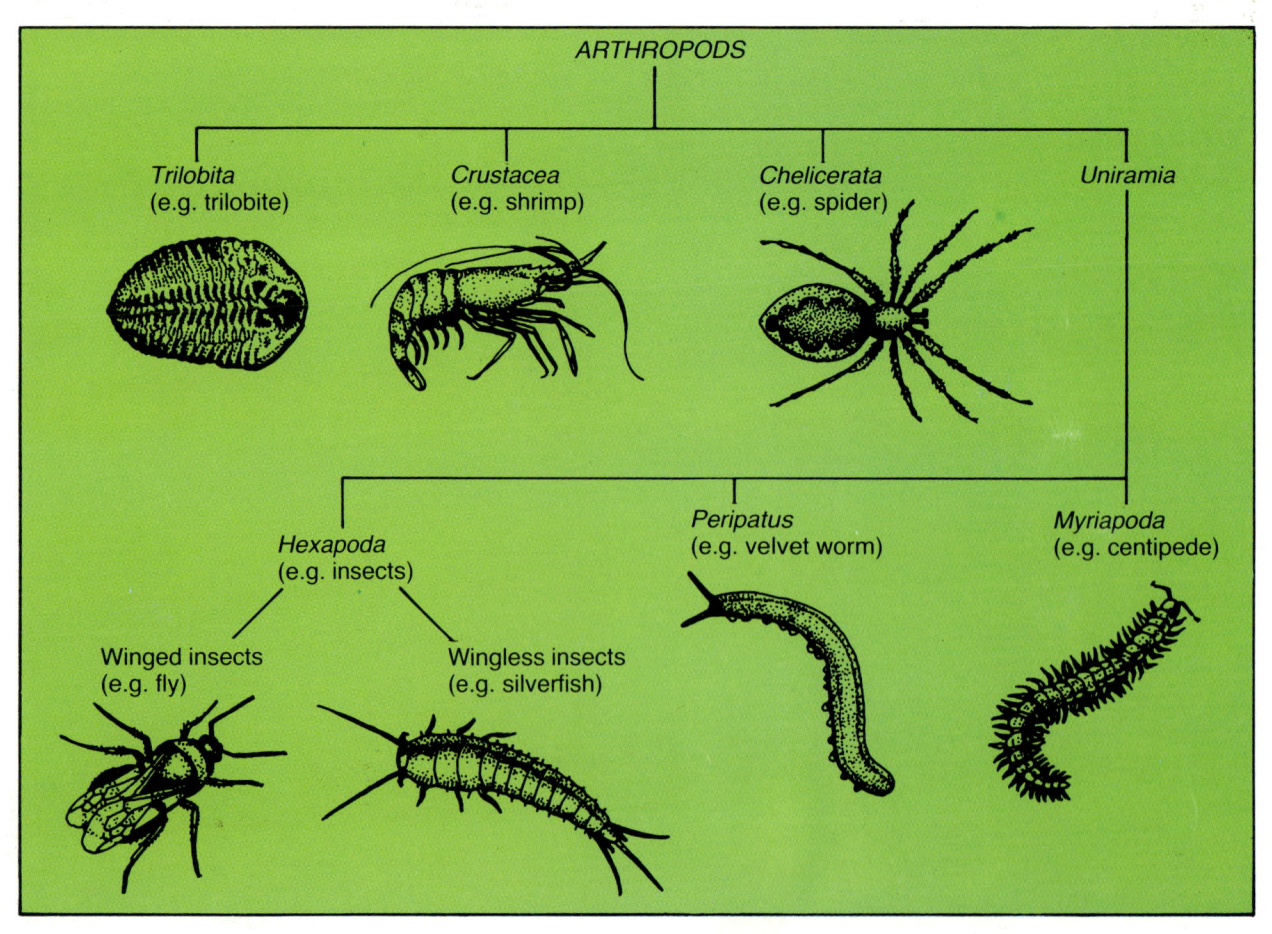

ARTHROPODS

Trilobita (e.g. trilobite)

Crustacea (e.g. shrimp)

Chelicerata (e.g. spider)

Uniramia

Hexapoda (e.g. insects)

Peripatus (e.g. velvet worm)

Myriapoda (e.g. centipede)

Winged insects (e.g. fly)

Wingless insects (e.g. silverfish)

What is an Insect?

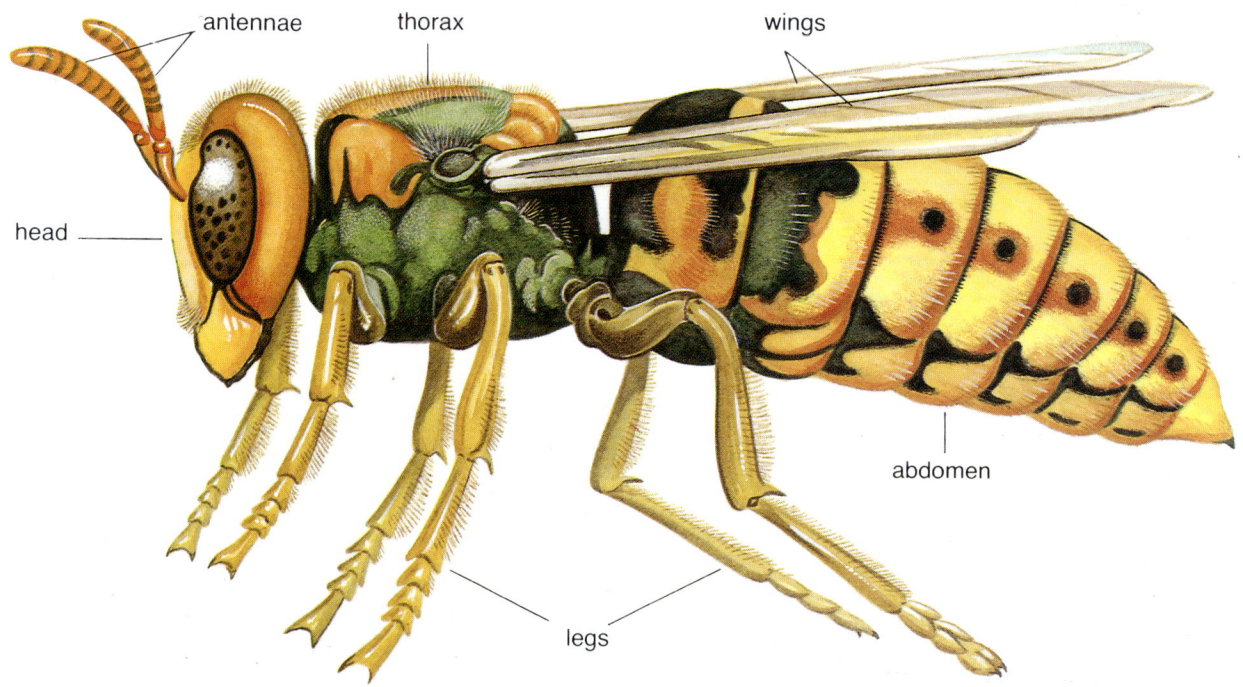

Labels on illustration: antennae, thorax, wings, head, abdomen, legs

Keeping Warm

Insects are **cold-blooded** animals. This means that they warm up or cool down as the weather changes. Many animals, like humans, are **warm-blooded**. We keep our bodies at a steady heat by using food as fuel.

Insects must be warm enough to be able to fly or move quickly. One way of getting warm is to sunbathe. Many insects are dark in color to help them soak up heat from the sun. Dark colors absorb heat better than pale colors.

Many insects pass the winter by keeping still, or **hibernating**. This is their way of living through cold weather. Insects which live in warm parts of the world are active all year. Their problem may be that they get too hot. Desert insects often have long legs to keep their bodies off the hot sand.

▲ All insects have three main parts. The head is the insect's control center. The thorax is the power plant. The abdomen contains the stomach.

▶ In the winter, it is too cold for many insects to lead an active life. These seven-spot ladybugs have huddled together and will not become active again until the weather is warm.

Before the Dinosaurs

Insects have lived on earth for a very long time. The remains, or **fossils**, of the very first insects are found in rocks. They are over 350 million years old.

The First Insects

The first insects had no wings. Their bodies were made up of a head, thorax, and abdomen. They probably fed on dead bits of plants. Fossils of later insects show that some grew small bumps on their thorax. These are thought to be the start of wings and helped the insects to glide.

Three hundred million years ago the world was covered by warm swamps full of plants. These made good homes for all types of insects.

Most of these insect types had wings. Some of them looked like dragonflies. They had wings up to 2 feet 6 inches across. These monster insects are not found today. They did, however, give rise to modern dragonflies.

▼ Insects have been flying on earth for about 300 million years. Fossils of early insects tell us that some were huge. The ones that looked like this dragonfly had wingspans as long as an adult human being's arm.

Before the Dinosaurs

Insects as Fossils

Insect fossils are not often found. Most insects are eaten or fall to pieces before they can turn into fossils. Long ago, the few that fell into mud on the bottom of lakes became fossils. A very few were buried by ash from volcanoes.

Over millions of years this mud and ash became rock. Only the hard parts of the insects remained in the rocks. The thin wings and fine hairs are left as outlines.

By far the best insect fossils are found in a rock called amber. Amber looks like yellow glass. It is made from the **sap** that oozed from pine trees millions of years ago. Insects fed on this sap. Some were trapped because the sap was sticky. The oldest insect fossils found in amber are over 70 million years old.

Survival Through the Ages

Insects are one of the most successful animal groups. Some of those we see today are much like some that lived long ago. Ants which have been found in amber look just like types living now.

Very few other animal types have stayed the same over the ages. Most died out, or became **extinct**, as new types appeared.

▲ The insects in this piece of amber have been there for millions of years. Some types no longer exist, but others have hardly changed. Over half of the types of ants found in amber still exist.

Such animals could not change with their changing world. One of the secrets to the insect's success is that they can cope with changes. Most of the insects we see were here when humans appeared on earth.

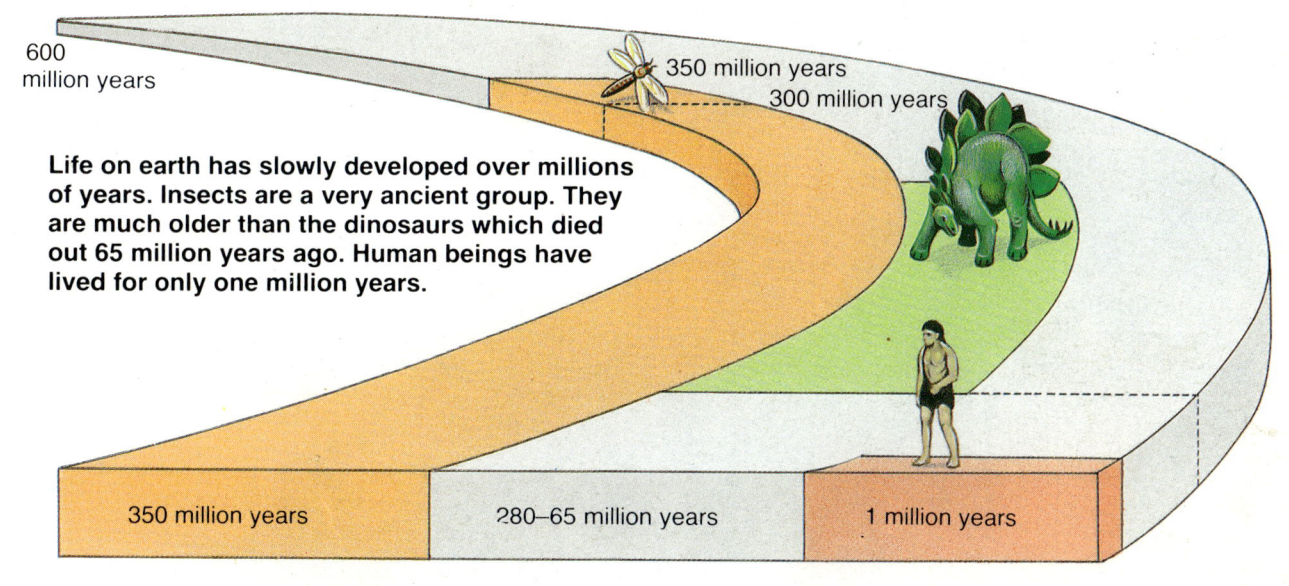

600 million years

350 million years
300 million years

Life on earth has slowly developed over millions of years. Insects are a very ancient group. They are much older than the dinosaurs which died out 65 million years ago. Human beings have lived for only one million years.

| 350 million years | 280–65 million years | 1 million years |

Thousands of Types

There are more different types of insects today than all the other animals put together. Three out of four animals are insects. Almost one million types are known and more are found all the time.

Insects also exist in the greatest numbers. One beehive may have 50,000 bees. Even so, many people do not notice insects because they are so small.

Why are there so many different insects? Insects live and feed on plants. There are thousands of different plants. As plants have changed, insects have changed too. They have had to in order to survive. So there are thousands of different insects, too.

Insects in Groups

Insects are divided into groups. There are about 30 groups called **orders**. An example of an order is the **Lepidoptera** (*Lep-e-dop-ter-a*), which includes all butterflies and moths.

Some of the orders contain lots of insects. The beetle order has over 300,000 types. To help sort out smaller groups, each order is then divided into families. For instance, the stag beetles make up one family.

It is sometimes hard to tell insect types apart. However, each type, or **species**, differs in shape, color or **habits** from all other insects.

▼ Scientists have found that some types of insects are closely related to each other. They have placed these types into groups. A few of these groups are shown.

Wingless insects

Name	Where they live	Name	Where they live	Name	Where they live
Springtails	In the soil	Bristletails	In the soil	Silverfish	In leaves and houses

Winged insects with three life stages

Name	Where they live	Name	Where they live
Mayflies	The larvae live in water, the adults fly	Grasshoppers and crickets	Among plants
Dragonflies and damselflies	The larvae live in water, the adults fly free	Leaf and stick insects	Among plants
Roaches and mantids	Among plants, dead leaves and in buildings	Book lice	Among dead plants
Termites	In huge nests of soil	True lice	On animals (parasites)
Earwigs	Among plants	Biting lice	On animals (parasites)
Stoneflies	The larvae live in water, the adults fly free	True bugs	On animals, among plants or in water
		Thrips	Among plants

Winged insects with four life stages

Name	Where they live	Name	Where they live
Alderflies and snakeflies	Among plants and in water	Beetles	Everywhere
Lacewings and ant lions	Among plants and on the ground	True flies	Everywhere
Scorpion flies	Among plants and in the soil	Caddis flies	The larvae in water, the adults fly
Fleas	On animals (parasites) and in rubbish	Butterflies and moths	Among plants
		Bees, ants, and wasps	Among plants and on the ground

Thousands of Types

Making Changes

All insect species live in one kind of place. If food runs out or their living space changes, they must adapt, too. If they do not adapt they will die. The simplest change an insect can make is to change its color.

A color change happened in a black and white moth called a peppered moth. The pattern of this moth changed in just over 100 years. This change happened because the tree trunks it rested on became black from factory smoke. These moths like to hide on trees. The wings of the moth changed to black, so it could not be seen easily. This type of moth became more common than the old black and white speckled form.

A faster change happened with insect **pests**. Pests are a menace to humans. Humans began to use poisons to kill them about 50 years ago. Now these poisons do not work. Insects such as mosquitoes and roaches have learned to resist them.

▲ There are two peppered moths on the tree. A bird would attack the black one. If the tree were black, the speckled one would be eaten.

▼ Notice the male and female mosquito. The male has feathery antennae.

Insect Skeletons

The **exoskeleton**, or skin, of an insect is light and strong. It can bend into all sorts of shapes. Insects come in almost any shape you could imagine.

A Suit of Armor

The insect skin is made from a very strong material called **chitin**. It is like a suit of armor. There are many sections which are joined to each other by a form of this thin material which can bend.

Unlike bony skeletons, the exoskeleton cannot grow with the insect. The only way an insect can grow is to shed its old skin and grow a larger new one. This is called **molting**. It can happen up to ten times in the life of an insect.

When an insect molts, it first grows a new soft skin under the old one. Then the old skin breaks open. The insect pulls itself free of the old skin. It has to let the new one dry out and harden.

◀ A new skin! A dragonfly molts up to 10 times in its life and gets slightly bigger each time. The old skin still clings to the plant. When the new skin is hard, the dragonfly will fly away.

▼ This is the middle part of an insect's body. The hard outside skeleton is the frame of the insect. Muscles are attached to the frame.

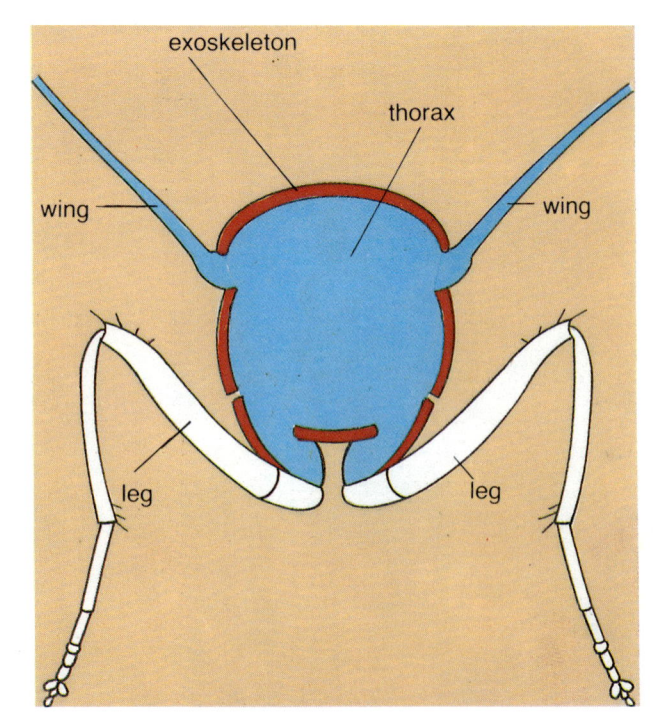

Insect Skeletons

Many Parts

When we look closely at an insect we see that each of the three main parts has a different job to do. The head is used to find and eat food. The **thorax** is the powerhouse. It holds the legs and wings. The **abdomen** holds all the parts dealing with digesting food and laying eggs.

A closer look at the abdomen shows us that it is made up of many sections called **segments**. Each segment is jointed to the next. This helps the insect to move the abdomen in all directions. The head and thorax are also made up of segments, but they are difficult to see.

Insect Hairs

The outside of an insect's body is covered by tiny hairs. Moths have soft hair which keeps them warm while flying. Some hairs act like tiny fingers which feel the ground. Insects use special hairs to smell or taste. Other tiny hairs tell the insect how damp the air is. Mosquitoes have hairs which act like ears. They can hear the hum of other mosquitoes.

▲ Look at a caterpillar eating a cotton plant. You can see the segments on the body which allow the insect to bend.

▼ This is the leg of a bee magnified 480 times! The skin of an insect is hard and cannot feel things as our skin does. Instead, thousands of hairs pass messages to the insect's brain.

How Insects Move

Insects move by using their legs or wings. Most types of insects have long legs. These are used to walk or run. Some have specially shaped legs which are used to swim, jump, or dig. All insect legs are made up of five main parts. This helps them to bend. Legs always come in pairs. Each pair can look different than the others.

Insect Flight

Most insects have two pairs of wings. Some only have one pair, and a few have no wings at all. Each insect wing has a skeleton of tubes called **veins**. They make the wing strong but light. A thin "skin" is stretched over the veins. This is made of the same material as the **exoskeleton**.

How does an insect fly? Powerful muscles in the insect's body make the insect's wings flap up and down. Each wing pushes down on the air beneath. This makes the insect go upwards into the air. Some insects beat their wings very fast. This often makes a humming noise.

Many insects fly very fast. Others, such as butterflies, fly quite slowly. Most insects with two pairs of wings have the front ones joined to the back ones so they beat together. This helps them to fly better. Insects with one pair of wings fly the fastest. Wings are very important to insects. Flight helps them to escape from their enemies. Flight also helps them to find food quickly. Flying, however, uses lots of energy. This means that insects need lots of food.

Some insects fly thousands of miles. This is called **migration**. Some do this to escape the cold winters. Others do it to escape dry weather.

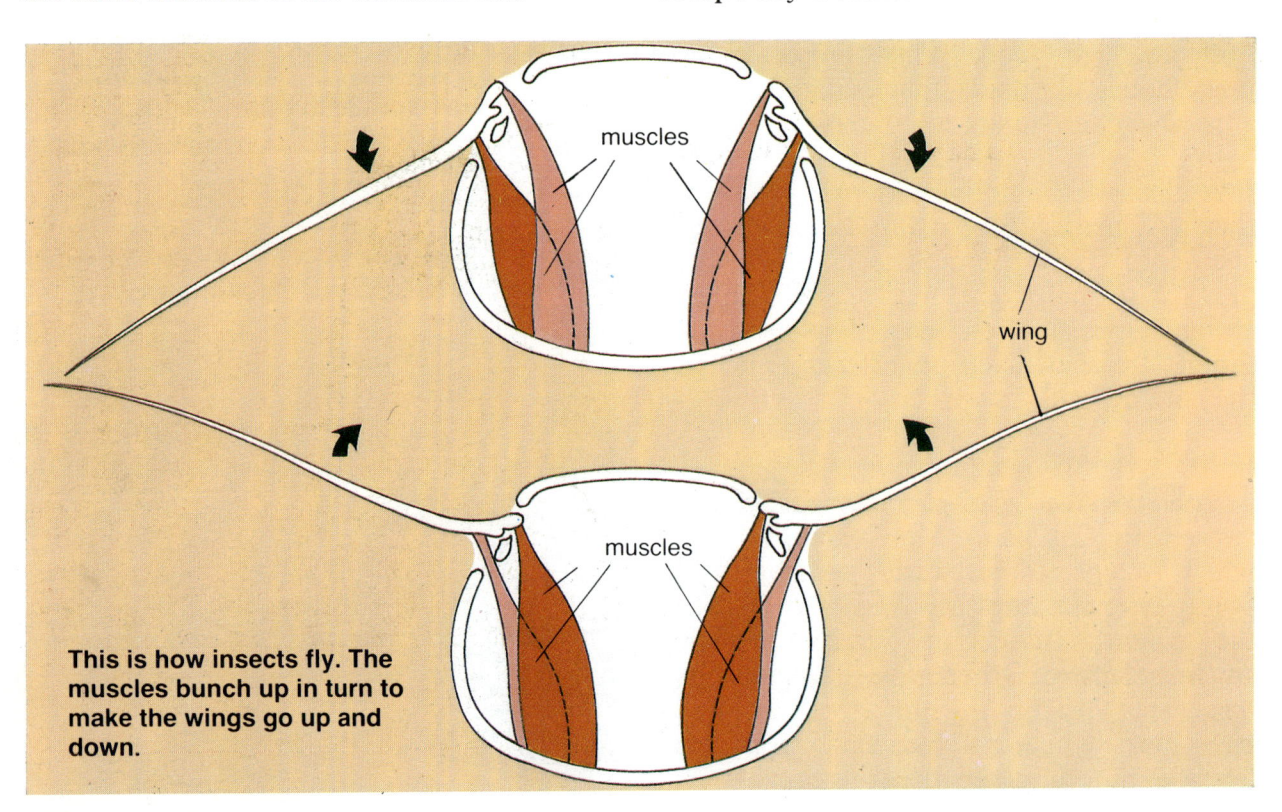

This is how insects fly. The muscles bunch up in turn to make the wings go up and down.

How Insects Move

▲ Three pictures taken in less than a second help to show how this yellow underwing moth flies.

▶ A pond skater walks on water by spreading its weight on long thin legs.

Insect Feet and Legs

You can learn a lot about how an insect moves by looking at its legs. If the legs are thin, the insect probably runs. If they are fat and hairy, the insect might swim.

Insects that dig have large front legs which look much like shovels. Some insects live inside wood. They make their burrows by eating into the wood as they go. They do not have legs, so they move along the tunnels by wriggling.

Some insects, such as fleas or crickets, are terrific leapers. They have very strong legs. The flea is the best jumper in the animal world. If it were as big as a human, it could jump over a skyscraper.

Seeing and Feeling

The insect world is very different from ours. Insects do not see colors or shapes in the same way we do. Some only see light or dark. Insects do not have noses or tongues like we do. They have very different ways of tasting and smelling.

Sight

Insects have two types of eyes. Most young insects, called **larvae**, have up to ten small eyes. These are called simple eyes. They tell the insect if it is night or day. Simple eyes cannot see shapes.

Most adult insects have a pair of large eyes called **compound eyes**. Each eye is made up of many tiny **lenses**. Each lens can only see part of the view around the insect. By using lots of lenses the insect sees the whole picture.

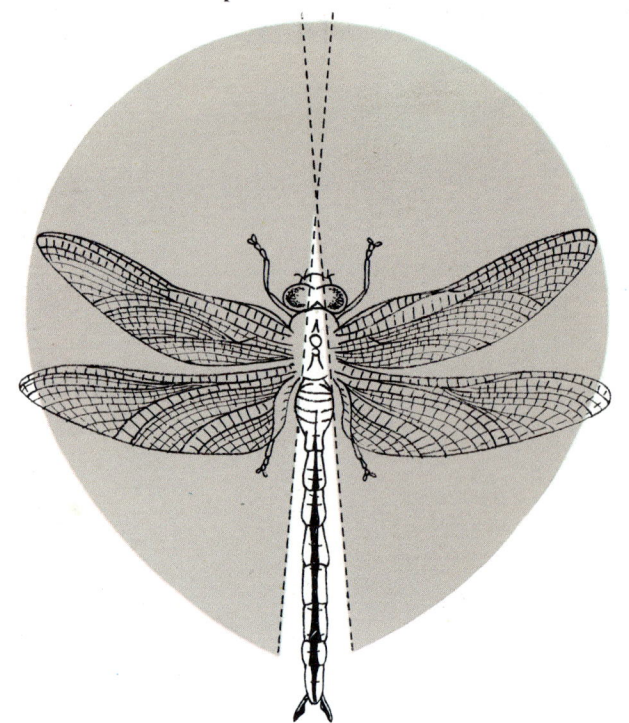

▲ This compound eye of a peacock butterfly has been magnified 75 times. The eye is surrounded by hairs, which help to keep the insect warm.

◀ The shaded area shows that insects can see almost all around them without moving.

Compound eyes stick out from the head of the insect. This allows it to see above, behind, and below. The lenses of the insect eye cannot move. This means that insects are very poor at judging distances, since they cannot **focus**.

Few animals are able to see in color, but most insects do. They use color patterns to recognize their own type. Each type of insect has its own color pattern. Insects can see a special color of light called **ultraviolet**. Many flowers have ultraviolet patterns. Since we cannot see ultraviolet light, these patterns are invisible to us.

Seeing and Feeling

Feeling, Tasting and Smelling

Insects are often hairy animals. Some of their hairs serve special purposes. They are used for feeling, tasting, and smelling. Very stiff hairs are called bristles. These are often found on the legs of insects. Each time a bristle touches the ground it bends. A tiny **nerve** at the base of the bristle feels this bending and tells the insect where it is safe to walk.

▼ Face to face with a luna moth! The eyes are the two dark patches. The two antennae look like green feathers.

Flying insects have thin hairs on their foreheads which bend in the wind. They tell the insect how fast it is flying. Hairs for smelling are often found on the feelers, or **antennae**. Different types of insects have different shapes of antennae.

Hairs for tasting are usually found on the feet of insects. Flies taste sugar with their feet. Other insects have tasting hairs all over their bodies. Some insects have special patches of hairs which feel warmth. These are used by insects which feed on blood. They can find animals by the heat they produce.

Breathing and Feeding

All adult animals feed to stay alive. Food is turned into energy. To do this, animals need to breathe. They take in a gas from the air called **oxygen**. It is used to "burn" food. Breathing also helps to remove a waste gas called **carbon dioxide**.

Breathing

Animals such as cows, mice, and humans have **lungs**. They breathe by sucking air into the lungs. The blood system then carries oxygen through the body.

Insects do not have lungs. Instead they have lots of tiny tubes inside their bodies. Each tube connects to the outside air by openings on the side of the insect. These openings are called **spiracles**. From the spiracles each tube branches like a tree. Air taken in moves slowly down these tubes. Oxygen passes into the insect. The waste gas moves into the smallest tubes. It then flows into the main tubes and out of the spiracles.

Many insects live in water. Some breathe by carrying a bubble of air. Others breathe, like fish, through **gills**. Water is sucked across the insect's gills. The oxygen from it passes into the insect.

▼ Insects have a network of tubes in their bodies which carry air. The air enters the body through tiny holes called spiracles. A spiracle, magnified 200 times, is shown in the lower right-hand corner.

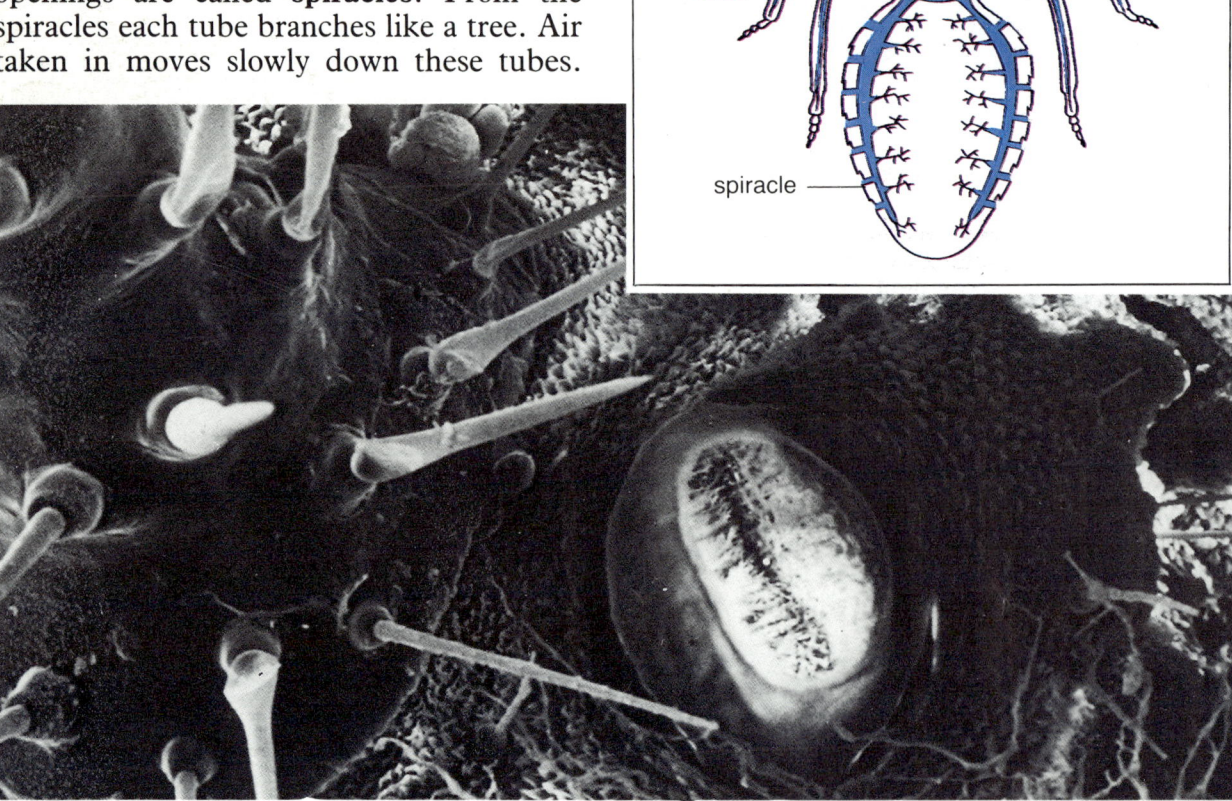

Breathing and Feeding

▲ A close-up of a tiger beetle's head. Its jaws, at the bottom of the picture, are very strong. The hard pointed tips cut up the insect's food.

Feeding

Insects have mouths like all animals. Most have a pair of sharp jaws called **mandibles**. These are used to cut up plants or flesh. Each mandible has a hard tip. Some insects have different ways of feeding. True bugs have a sucking mouth. Moths have a long coiled tube. A few insects do not feed at all when they are adults.

There are lots of insect types, and among them they eat almost anything. Most eat plants or wood. Some eat manure, hair, or skin. Many others feed on blood. Usually, each type of insect only eats one type of food. Their mouths are shaped to help them feed. Those which eat plants have sharp, cutting jaws. Blood-suckers have long hollow "needles."

Some insects eat many types of food. This lets them live in many kinds of places. Roaches and crickets can eat both plants and animals. Their mandibles are broad and strong.

To get energy from food the insect must **digest** it. First, food is taken into the mouth to be crushed. Then it passes along to the stomach. There the nourishment is taken out. The useless parts of food are **excreted** as droppings.

A Life Cycle

A **life cycle** is the name we give to the changes that an animal goes through, from egg to adult. There are two kinds of insect life cycles. One has three **stages**: egg, **nymph**, and adult. The other has four stages: egg, **larva, pupa,** and adult.

At each stage the insect has a different shape. Eggs are easy to tell from the other stages. The eggs have a tough shell. This keeps the tiny larvae inside safe. Once they have hatched, the larvae grow by changing their skins. An insect usually has four or five sizes of larva. Each one may vary in color or shape. Insect larvae are given many names. These include grub, nymph, or caterpillar. The name depends upon the shape of the larva. Some insects have a resting stage called a pupa. This stage is between the larva and the adult.

The Life of a Grasshopper

A grasshopper has three stages in its life cycle. It grows from an egg to an adult in a few months. The eggs are laid in sandy soil. They may stay there all winter and hatch in late spring. They are protected by a layer of hard **foam secreted** by the grasshopper. The young grasshoppers are called nymphs. Most go through four skin changes.

▼ **The life cycle of a grasshopper has three stages: egg, nymph, and adult. The life cycle of a butterfly has four: egg, larva, pupa, and adult.**

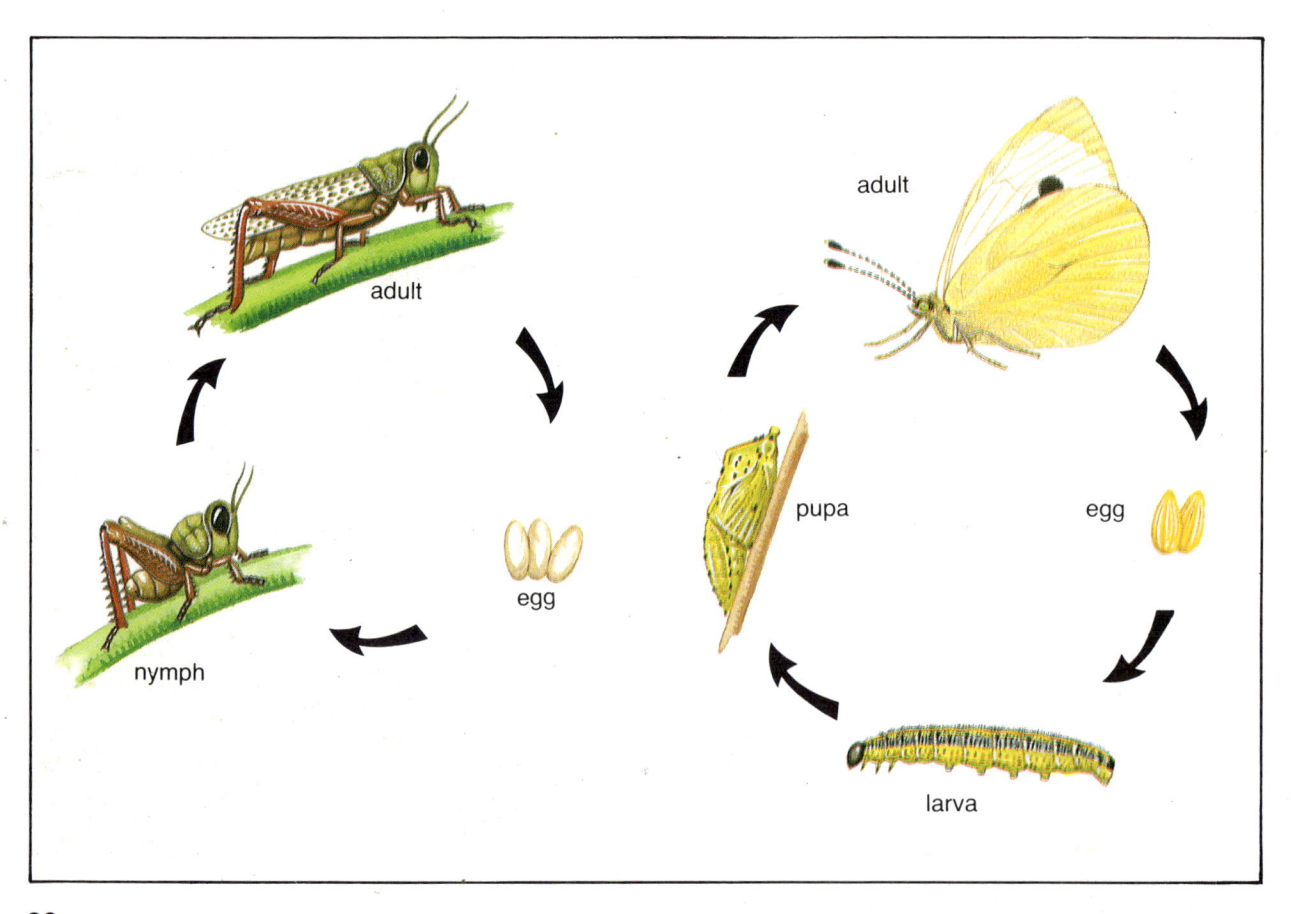

A Life Cycle

All sizes of nymphs look like adults without wings. After the fourth skin change, the nymph becomes an adult. The grasshopper never changes its skin again. Adults live up to five months. They spend their lives feeding, mating, and laying eggs.

The Life of a Butterfly

A butterfly's life cycle has four stages. A full cycle takes a year. Most eggs hatch about ten days after being laid. A few butterflies lay eggs which live through the winter. The butterfly larva is called a caterpillar. Each caterpillar has five skin changes. During each change they may also alter their color.

Once fully grown, the caterpillar changes into a pupa. The pupa is protected by a **cocoon**. After a week or so the cocoon breaks open. A perfect butterfly crawls out. It unfolds its wings to dry them out. Most butterflies only live for a week.

▲ These eggs of a cabbage butterfly are magnified many times. These butterflies lay their eggs on leaves. When they hatch into caterpillars, they have food nearby.

▼ Here we see four honeybees during the pupa stage. The one on the left is the oldest and will soon become an adult.

Insects Everywhere

Most insects live on land or in fresh water. A few types live in the sea. Some live in very cold places while others live in hot deserts. Insects are everywhere, from the deepest lakes to the highest mountains.

Where Insects Live

Most insects live on plants. The largest number of plants are found in forests. Forests in hot countries are very good places for insects to live. A single plant can be a home for many different insects. A tree can be home for millions of them. Some eat flowers; others eat roots or leaves.

At each stage of its life, an insect may live in a different place. Some larvae live inside flat leaves. They are called leaf miners. The larva of an ant lion lives in sand. The adult lives in bushes.

▲ The larva of an ant lion digs a pit in sandy soil. Then, it waits with jaws wide open for an unlucky insect to tumble into its trap.

◀ This is a dune cricket from the Namib Desert, Africa. The insect's unusual feet prevent it from sinking into the sand. Note the long antennae and the coloring which helps to camouflage the insect.

Insects Everywhere

Some insects live in strange homes. A few types of insects live in caves in pure darkness. They are blind, since eyes would be of no use. Others live in salty lakes where no other animals survive.

One of the strangest insects is an African midge. The larvae live in pools which sometimes dry up. Then the larvae shrivel up. The dry midge larvae look like seeds. When the rains return, they swell up again and come to life. These larvae can stay dried up for twenty years and still come to life!

Survival of the Few

Insects lay lots of eggs. A female housefly can lay up to 2,000 eggs in her life. Each egg can grow into an adult in two weeks. If all the eggs that flies lay grew into adults, the world could not cope with their numbers. In three months the world would be covered in a layer of flies.

This does not happen because most eggs or larvae are eaten. Only a few ever survive to breed. Usually there is too little food. Many larvae starve to death. When there is plenty of food the insects quickly spread in huge numbers. Fields can provide lots of food. Many insects become **pests** in fields. Farmers have to kill them to save their crops.

Many insects are eaten by other animals. Some try to hide and escape being eaten. Others are colored, or **camouflaged**. They try to look like twigs or leaves. A few insects contain poisons. They are brightly colored to warn other animals. Their poisons help stop them from being eaten.

▼ Insects can multiply at a frightening rate. This tree will soon be stripped bare by the locusts that have landed on it. Locusts are among the most feared insect pests.

Insect Builders

Many insects build their own homes. Their homes help protect them from their enemies. The simplest insect homes are hollow plant stems. Insects often use these to store their food.

Most insects can make silk. Some, like the **caddis fly** larva, use silk to spin a case. This larva carries its colorful silk case around with it. Some caterpillars spin silk tents in which they spend the night. During the day they live on the outside so that they can feed.

Silk is also used to sew leaves together. Many caterpillars live in sewn up leaf rolls. This hides and protects them. A few kinds of ants sew leaves together to make a tent home.

Building Materials

Silk is not the only building material. Insects such as ants use twigs and leaves, which they gather into mounds. Other insects make their own "cement." They mix mud or soil with their **saliva**. This is then used to make nests or tubes.

The best soil builders are the termites. They are tiny insects, but they can build huge nests. Some of their nest mounds reach over twenty feet in height. Millions of termites live in each nest.

Other insects build with wood. Wasps chew up wood into **pulp**. This makes a type of paper. They use this to build their nests.

Bumblebees and honeybees make their own wax. They use the wax to make perfect **honeycombs** inside a hollow tree or hole.

◀ Weaver ants at work. These amazing creatures put leaves together to make nests. They use a sticky silk thread that is produced by their larvae. The silk thread glues the leaves together. You can see a larva being held by one of the ants in the middle of the picture.

Insect Builders

Ant City

Many ants build mounds above the ground. These are really the roof for the nest. Inside the nest are thousands of ants. Each ant has its own special job to do. Some ants gather food outside the nest. Others feed the larvae. The success of the whole nest depends on all the ants working together.

The nest contains tunnels with spaces. Each space, or **chamber**, is used to keep eggs, larvae, or food. Each nest has one queen ant. She has her own chamber. Her life is spent producing millions of eggs. These eggs are carried to other chambers by **worker ants**. When the eggs hatch into larvae, they are looked after and fed.

◀ It is hard to believe that small insects such as termites can build tall mounds like this one in Southern Africa. The mound is ten feet tall, and it contains thousands of termites.

▼ A network of tunnels joins the chambers of an ant nest. In one chamber, the queen lays her eggs. In the others, the young are looked after.

Bees and Wasps

There are thousands of types of bees and wasps. Most of them live alone. Each builds its own nest burrow in plants or soil. Each nest is filled with food to feed the **larva** once it is hatched.

Wasps and bees use many kinds of food. Some collect **pollen** or **nectar** from flowers; others catch spiders or **caterpillars**.

Bees are usually very hairy. They can be brown or striped. Wasps do not have hairy bodies. They are often striped black and yellow. All wasps have a very narrow "waist."

Living Together

Some bees and wasps build huge nests. Each may contain over 40,000 insects. These are called **social bees** or wasps.

Wild honeybees nest in hollow trees. Humans copy this by giving them wooden boxes called hives. Inside the hive the bees build nest **cells** from wax. A queen bee lays an egg in each cell. Each hive only has one queen bee. The eggs hatch into grubs which are fed by bees called **workers**. The worker bees also visit flowers to collect pollen and nectar for food.

▼ A queen honeybee (marked with the red dot) surrounded by some of her workers. They are standing on the empty cells into which the queen will lay eggs. The cells have been built by the workers.

Bees and Wasps

New nests are formed in summer. The queen bee leaves the old nest with lots of workers. This is called a **swarm**. She leads the swarm to a new hive or tree. Inside the old nest new queen bees are hatched. They leave the nest with male bees called **drones**. Only one queen returns to the old nest after mating. She takes over the egg laying to keep the nest going.

Some of the nest cells are used for food. These are filled with honey which will be eaten by the bees over the winter.

Wasp nests also have a queen. The worker wasps catch other insects for food. They feed these to their larvae. New queen wasps hatch in late summer. They mate and hide away for the winter. All the other wasps die as winter comes.

Jobs for All

All bees or wasps in a nest know what their jobs are. Some feed and care for the larvae. Others clean out the garbage. Many workers fly out in search for food.

The queen keeps the nest together. She produces a special scent or chemical. This is passed from adult to adult in food. This scent stops the workers from trying to lay eggs.

▲ A swarm of honeybees rests while scouts search for a new nest. Buried in this swarm will be a single queen. She has left her old nest because a new queen has hatched there.

▶ Social wasps, or yellow-jackets, are on a nest. Eggs and larvae can be seen in the nest cells.

Butterflies and Moths

Butterflies and moths belong to the same group of insects. How do they differ? Butterflies usually fly in the day. Moths usually fly at night. Most butterflies are brightly colored. They have **antennae** with knobs at the tips. Moths are often a brownish color. Their antennae can be feathery or straight.

Look at the butterfly (above) and the moth (below). Note that the antennae are very different. The small diagrams show the butterfly and moth at rest. The butterfly rests with its wings closed. The moth rests with wings open.

Avoiding Enemies

The wings of butterflies and moths are covered with tiny **scales**. Lots of scales help to form a pattern on the wings. The scales lie on the wing like tiles on a roof. Each butterfly and moth has a different pattern. Some look like leaves, while others match tree bark or rocks. These patterns help them to avoid their enemies.

Butterflies rest with their wings closed over their backs. In this position, the leaf pattern is visible on the wings. When they spread their wings, they are often brightly colored. Bright colors help butterflies to recognize their relatives.

Moths rest with their wings held flat. They have their hiding patterns on the top part of the wings. Moths use scents to find their relatives. Bright colors are useless at night!

Butterflies and Moths

Many brightly colored insects are poisonous. Their patterns and colors warn birds of this fact. Butterflies and moths get their poisons from plants. Birds soon learn not to eat brightly colored insects.

Not all brightly colored butterflies are poisonous. Some copy the patterns of other poisonous butterflies. These copycat butterflies are called **mimics**. Birds do not eat them because of their color. Mimic butterflies must not become too common. If they do, then birds might discover their trickery!

▼ The bright colors of this monarch butterfly caterpillar warn birds not to eat it. In nature, bright colors mean poison. Some insects pretend to be poisonous, but this caterpillar really is!

▲ A close-up of the wing of a peacock butterfly shows it is covered with thousands of tiny scales. The scales join together to form a complete picture, or pattern, like the dots on a television screen. Each scale can be a different color.

A Warning in Colors

Not all butterflies and moths look like leaves or rocks. Many are brightly colored in reds, yellows, or blues. Even caterpillars have brightly striped coats.

Some moths hide their bright colors. If attacked by a bird they suddenly open their wings. A bright flash of red or yellow scares the bird. Such patterns are called **flash colors**.

Some butterflies and moths have patterns on their wings that look like eyes. These eye spots are there to scare and trick birds.

29

Crickets and Their Relatives

Crickets, grasshoppers, and locusts make up one insect group. They all have strong back legs which they use for jumping. Some grasshoppers and locusts can also fly well.

Most crickets eat both plants and animals. They can be found in bushes and on the ground. A small number, called mole crickets, live in the soil.

Crickets usually have long **antennae** and small wings. They live in warm parts of the world. House crickets live in houses all over the world.

Grasshoppers and locusts live in fields. They have short antennae and most have long wings over their backs. Those that cannot fly use their wings to glide. All grasshoppers have two pairs of wings. The front ones, which are like leather, cover the thin back ones when at rest.

Grasshoppers and locusts are colored green or brown to help them hide among plants. Some are colored dark brown to help them soak up heat from the sun. Once they are warmed up, they can jump quickly and fly fast.

▲ A grasshopper is feeding on a flower. Its strong back legs are armed with spikes. If it is attacked, the grasshopper lashes out and jumps away.

Insect Musicians

How do grasshoppers and crickets make their well-known sounds? Grasshoppers make sounds by rubbing their legs over a tough **vein** on their front wing. A violin's sound is made by the bow rubbing over the strings. The grasshopper's leg is his bow. The wing vein is the string.

How a grasshopper (left) and a cricket (right) make sounds.

Crickets and Their Relatives

When crickets make sounds they use only their wings. One wing has a thick vein with bumps along it. This is called the **file**. It is rubbed over a tough ridge on the other wing. This produces the cricket song. A relative of the cricket has a song that sounds like 'katy-did-she-did'. This has given it the name katydid.

Locusts

Locusts are really just big grasshoppers. Some kinds are found in fields and others live in deserts. They do damage to crops in warm parts of the world. The desert locust can live alone or in **swarms**. A single swarm can contain millions of locusts. Swarms appear when there has been plenty of food.

The young locusts are called **hoppers**, because of the way they move. When many hoppers come together we say that they band together. Huge bands of hoppers can cover vast areas. They eat everything in their path.

When they become adults, they fly away in swarms. Each locust is an eating machine. Swarms soon eat themselves out of food. Most of them die of starvation.

▼ Most of us would not be very happy walking through a swarm of noisy locusts. This man is either brave or used to it.

One Pair of Wings

The name "fly" is used for many insects. True flies only have one pair of wings. All other insects either have two pairs or none at all. Butterflies and dragonflies are not true flies. They belong to different insect groups.

There are 85,000 different types of true flies. Each uses front wings to fly. Instead of back wings they have tiny knobs which look like drumsticks. The knobs are called **halteres** (*hal-tir-ez*). They help to steady the fly as it flies.

Flies come in all shapes and sizes. The tiniest are a fraction of an inch long and the largest have wings up to about 3 inches across. They are often very bristly. Each fly's body is clearly divided into three parts. The head may have huge eyes. The **thorax** is square and tough. The **abdomen** can be quite long and is sometimes brightly colored.

Many flies have tiny antennae. These can be bristly or end in a knob. All true flies have mouths which suck. Some have short mouths for sucking **nectar**. Others have mouths like needles for feeding on the blood of other animals.

All true flies have four stages in their **life cycle**: egg, larva, pupa, and adult. Fly larvae are called grubs, or **maggots**, which are usually soft and pale. They have no legs and move by wriggling. Each type of larva is shaped to suit its way of life. Mosquito larvae are hairy. They live just under the surface of the water. **Midge** larvae look like worms. They live in the mud of ponds. Larvae of **hoverflies** have strong jaws. They eat aphids on plants.

▼ Is this just another fly you swat, or a really fine creature? As the blowfly basks in the sun, its thin wings shine with greens and pinks.

One Pair of Wings

A few of the many types of fly. All the flies here are adults. All adult flies have one pair of wings. The names of most flies give clues to their habits. For example, a hoverfly can hover and a horsefly bites horses.

The Biters

Many types of flies bite to feed on blood. Horseflies are very large biting flies. They buzz loudly and usually bite cows or horses. Tiny flies called buffalo gnats also bite. A few biters pass on diseases. Mosquitoes, in some warm parts of the world, carry a disease called **malaria**. It is a disease which can kill people.

Flies do not sting. Certain types look like wasps or bees, which helps them to fool birds. The flies that look like wasps are **mimics**. They even sound like wasps. However, all wasps have two pairs of wings, but the wasp-like flies only have one pair.

▶ The head of a horsefly. A horsefly is a large biting fly. The enormous eyes take up most of the head. There are 2,500 types of horseflies.

True Bugs and Beetles

Many of the true bugs and beetles look alike, but they can be told apart. All bugs have mouths like needles, and all beetles have biting mouths.

There are 40,000 types of bugs. They feed mostly on plant juices and a few feed on blood. The largest bug, the giant water bug, is over 4 inches long. It lives in water.

Aphids and cicadas (*ci-ka-das*) are plant bugs. They feed on the sweet **sap** of plants or trees. Another type of plant bug is called a spittlebug. Its larvae, called **nymphs**, live inside a ball of froth. This is often called cuckoo spit. It hides the larvae from their enemies.

Bedbugs and assassin bugs feed on blood. They bite other animals with their sharp mouths. Some types carry disease.

Meat-eaters

Beetles make up the largest insect group. There are over 300,000 types of beetle that come in all shapes. The largest goliath beetles can grow to six inches long. Almost all beetles have very hard front wings. These are useless for flying. These wings cover most of the body. They protect the delicate hind wings which are used for flying.

Most beetles eat plants, but some eat other insects. Meat-eating beetles have huge jaws. Most meat-eaters are called ground beetles. They are usually black and have long legs.

The fiercest meat-eaters are the tiger beetles, which are beautifully colored. The adult has large curved jaws. Tiger beetles can run very fast, and most can fly. Their larvae live in holes on flat ground. Each larva sits with its mouth wide open. Its jaws are like spring traps. Passing insects are snapped up as they walk over the hole.

◀ Assassin bugs attack and eat other insects. The prey here is a bee.

True Bugs and Beetles

Plant-eaters

Beetles can eat almost anything. The plant-eaters are most common. The Colorado beetle eats potato leaves and causes lots of damage to crops. Beetles called weevils are also pests.

The larvae of many beetles eat wood. Those of the longhorn beetle bore into trees. Stag beetle larvae eat rotten wood. Some types feed beneath bark or in twigs.

One beetle that does a valuable job is the **dung** beetle. The adults bury balls of dung. This is used as food by their larvae. Similar beetles feed on dead animals. They are called burying beetles. They bury dead mice and other small animals. Both of these types of beetles help clear the world of dead animal bodies and dung.

▶ Blister beetles should be left alone. If you touch these beetles, your skin will blister.

▼ A tiger beetle with prey. Tiger beetles move quickly. Unlike many other beetles, they are good fliers.

Water Insects

Many insects live in fresh water. Most prefer ponds or rivers, but a few live in fast-flowing streams. Water can be a good place to live. It contains lots of small animals and plants which insects eat.

A pond is home for many types of insects. Some, like the water strider, can walk on the surface. Mosquito larvae hang from the water surface. They have long hairs which spread out and stop them from sinking.

Swimming insects live below the surface. They use their flat, hairy legs as tiny oars. The water boatmen swim upside down. They have a pair of long legs like oars.

The muddy bottom of the pond is home for crawling insects. They also clamber over rocks and water plants.

Most water insects are larvae. Once they become adults they fly above the water. Mayfly and damselfly larvae use **gills** to breathe. Caddis fly larvae usually live inside silk cases. Each case is decorated with stones or sticks.

▼ Many kinds of insects can be found under the water or on the surface of ponds.

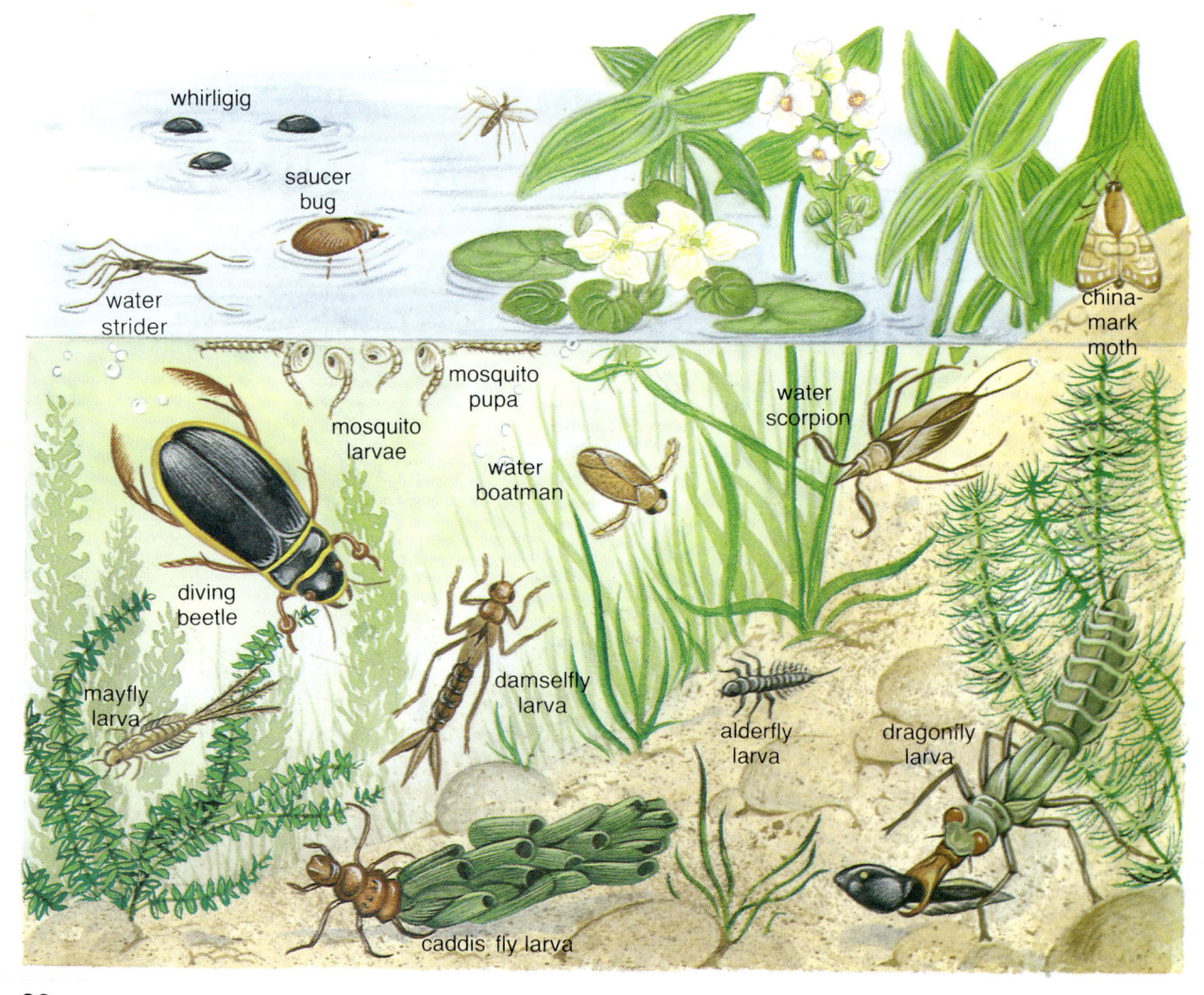

Water Insects

▲ After dragonflies become adults, they never return to live in water.

The Watery Jungle

Underwater insects are often meat-eaters. They catch and eat other small water animals. Some, such as the diving beetles, do so by swimming fast. Others use **camouflage** to wait for passing animals.

The water scorpion is a kind of true bug. It hides among the weeds. It has a long breathing tube. It uses this to suck air from above the water. The front legs of the water scorpion are used to grab food.

Some insect larvae have sharp jaws. The nymph of the Dobsonfly has huge curved **mandibles**. These snap tightly on its food.

Some water insects, like the water boatmen, look silvery. This is because they carry a small bubble of air with them. Many water beetles carry a silver bubble on their "tails."

Dragonflies

The dragonfly larva is a very strange creature. It feeds using a very special type of mouth. This is called a mask. The sharp mandibles are fixed to a bent "arm." This arm can be shot out to grab food.

Dragonfly larvae eat many types of animals. They can even catch small fish or tadpoles. They usually move very slowly, but if they are attacked they can escape at great speed. A stream of water can be squirted out of their bodies which shoots them forward.

Once it is fully grown the dragonfly larva leaves the water. It crawls up a plant stem and the winged adult emerges.

Unusual Insects

Insects may be called unusual for many reasons. They may have strange shapes, or they may live in very strange places. Insects are always trying to avoid being eaten. Many of the more unusual types are good at hiding. Others are unusual because of the way that they protect themselves.

Leaves and Sticks

Some of the most unusual insects live in Asia. They are the leaf and stick insects. They do not look like insects until they move.

Leaf insects have very flat, wide bodies. They even have blotches and pieces missing, just like a real leaf. During the day they stay quite still. They feed on leaves at night.

Stick insects can grow very large. An Australian type grows up to one foot long. They have long bodies that look like twigs. They are covered with bumps and spines, just like a real twig.

Stick insects are unusual for other reasons. Some types only seem to have females. The males are very rare. The females can lay eggs without mating. Other types pretend to be dead if attacked.

The young of some stick insects look like ants. This appearance protects them from birds. Real ants bite or sting, so the birds stay away.

◀ Stick insects are masters of disguise. They move slowly to avoid being seen. If one of their legs is broken off, they can grow another. Some types can change color to match their surroundings.

Unusual Insects

Living Thorns

An insect with a strange shape is the tree hopper. Tree hoppers are bugs which live in hot jungles. Some can look just like thorns. They even sit along twigs. The tree hoppers are green to match real thorns. Others are brightly colored. Even so, they do not look like insects until they move. They feed by sucking tree sap. Their good disguise keeps them safe from birds and lizards. Another strange bug is the lantern fly. Its head is very big and hollow. This was once thought to produce light, like a lantern.

Unusual Pairs

Male and female insects often look different. Many butterflies have brightly colored males and dull looking females. Some insects, however, have totally different males and females. There are female moths that do not have wings. They spend their short adult lives just laying eggs.

The glow worm female looks like its larva. The male glow worm looks like other beetles. It has a hard pair of front wings and can fly.

▲ Disguise yourself as a sharp thorn, and no enemy will try to eat you. This group of thornbugs includes nymphs and adults. The adults have larger "thorns," which give them better camouflage.

▼ These two very different looking insects are actually the male and female vaporer moths. The male is the one with wings.

female   male

Insects in Our Homes

The houses we live in are homes to many insects. There they find food and shelter. They eat all kinds of things in a house, from tiny leftovers to the house itself.

The types of insects that we find in our homes once lived in warm, dry places. Roaches came from hot countries. They were brought to colder countries by the first ships. They climbed aboard the ships without the sailors seeing them – like stowaways!

Other house insects, the clothes moths and silverfish, probably lived in old bird nests. In our houses they found a better, safer place to live. Dead trees once made a home for beetles that live in wood. They now find wooden tables and chairs to be much warmer homes.

Insects in Our Homes

Hidden from View

Insects find lots of hiding places in houses. They slip into cracks or below floors. They hide in the roof or under the carpets. We often never know that they are there.

Some only come out to feed at night. Roaches like the dark. They disappear if a light is turned on.

In the quiet of the night we can hear insect noises. The chirp of the house cricket tells us that it is there. The death watch beetle makes a tapping sound as its head knocks against its wooden tunnel.

◀ The woodworm, or common furniture beetle, is found in many homes. The floorboard shows the holes made by adult beetles. The larvae live inside the wood. They cause the most damage.

▼ Roaches feed on tainted food and pass on disease to our fresh food like this tomato. This is why we try to prevent insects from eating our food.

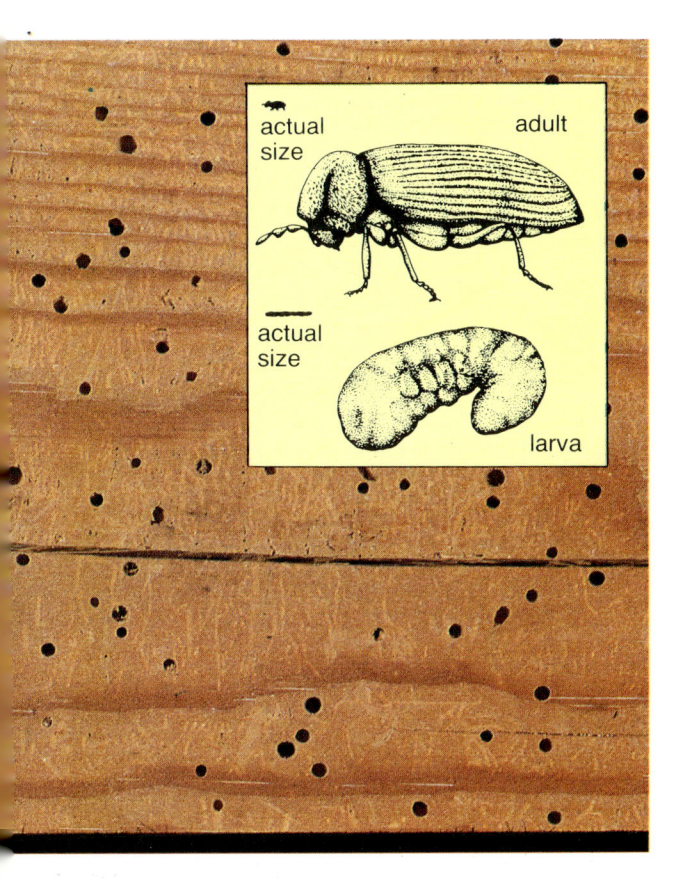

Food in Plenty

We do not find many house insects in the wild. The main reason for this is that there is plenty of food for them inside. Most houses contain lots of wood. This may be in the floor, in the walls, in the roof, or in tables and chairs. Many types of beetles eat wood. Some types eat so much that they can make a house fall down. They turn the hard wood that supports the house into dust.

Some house insects eat strange foods. Tiny book lice eat the glue which is used to glue books together. One beetle eats tobacco and cigarettes. Some insects even eat dust.

◀ A silverfish is feeding on breadcrumbs. This wingless insect is covered in silver scales, which makes it look like a fish. Silverfish are common house pests. They eat scraps, but they will eat books and even pictures on the walls.

41

Insects that Cause Harm

Insects upset our lives in many ways. They do this by eating our food and buildings and by spreading disease. Disease can kill humans and animals.

Humans wage constant war against insects. The most common weapons that humans use are chemical poisons. These are called **insecticides**. This means "insect killers." Some types of insects become used to these poisons. We say that they become **resistant**.

▶ Cabbage caterpillars feeding.

▼ This field of potatoes has been attacked by Colorado beetles. Spraying the field with insecticide could have prevented this attack.

Some insecticides, such as DDT, also poison other animals. This insecticide is not used today for this reason. Most insecticides also kill insects that help us, like bees. New types of insecticide kill one type of insect. In the future they will be used more and more. Do not worry; insects will always survive. They are more successful at living than humans.

Insects that Cause Harm

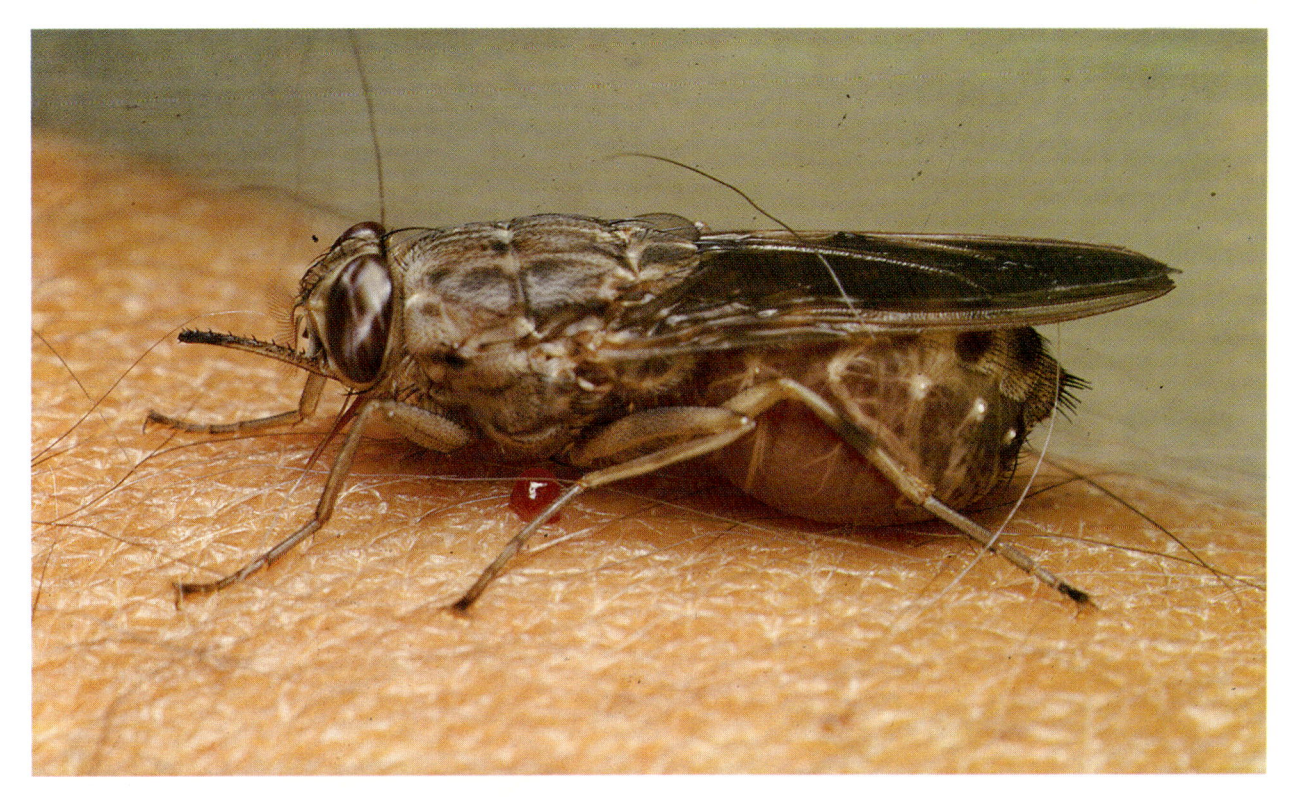

▲ A tsetse fly is feeding on human blood. Tsetse flies only feed as adults. The females give birth to fully grown larvae, instead of laying eggs. The larvae then change into adults.

Damage to Crops

Insects eat everything that humans grow. There are at least 125 types of insects which eat cotton plants. They do vast amounts of damage every year.

Locusts have always been pests. The Ancient Egyptians used to pay people to kill them. Today, they still cause damage to our crops. One of the worst pests today is the aphid. It kills plants by sucking the sap from them. Aphids also spread disease to plants.

Many insect pests are larvae. The caterpillars of cabbage butterflies eat cabbages, Brussels sprouts, and cauliflowers. Caterpillars of some moths can eat entire forests. Many plants have their roots eaten by insect larvae.

Carrying Disease

Some of the most dangerous diseases are spread by insects. Malaria, sleeping sickness, and yellow fever are all diseases passed on by insects.

Malaria is spread by female mosquitoes. They feed on blood and pass the disease into the human body. The disease lives in the blood and quickly spreads.

Sleeping sickness is a dangerous disease in Africa. It is carried by the tsetse (*tset-see*) fly. The female fly feeds on blood. She bites humans and animals.

Stopping the Damage

Insecticides are not the only means to stop the damage. Many insects eat other insects. In some countries insects which eat others are put into fields of crops by farmers. This is called **biological control**.

Many insects eat stored foods. This means that much food is lost. Better ways of storing food may stop this damage.

How Insects Help Us

▼ A honeybee hive is in an apple orchard. The bees are helping to make sure that a good crop of apples will grow here.

Not all insects eat crops. Some help us to grow them. The insects carry **pollen** on their hairs and feet as they move from flower to flower. Pollen makes a plant produce fruit or seeds. This is called **pollination**. In return, the flowers produce **nectar** for the insects. Butterflies, moths, beetles, and flies are all good pollinators. They all help our crops and flowers to make seeds. Our best insect friends are the bees. Honeybee hives are put in orchards to pollinate trees.

How Insects Help Us

Clothes and Food

Some of the finest clothes are made out of silk. The Chinese have used silk for over 4,000 years. Silk is produced by caterpillars of the silkworm moth. These moths are kept on special farms. The silkworms spin a tough case to protect themselves in the **pupa** stage. This is called a **cocoon**. Each cocoon is made from silk thread. The silk thread is taken by humans to make clothes.

The most famous insect food is honey. This is collected from the hives of honeybees. Honey is a mixture of nectar and pollen. The honeybees also produce beeswax, which we use for polishing wood. Beeswax was once used to make candles.

Insects are eaten as food in some countries. Ants, **termites**, and locusts are eaten in parts of Africa. Grubs and grasshoppers are eaten in some parts of Australia.

▲ A silk worm spins its cocoon in about five days. This cocoon is complete. The silk is taken before the adult moth can form inside.

◄ Insects can help in the control of plants. Young caterpillars are feeding on a prickly pear cactus.

Insect Helpers

Many insects help humans by eating pests. The ladybug is the farmer's friend. The **larvae** and adult ladybugs eat lots of **aphids**. Insects can be used to eat weeds — like tiny grass cutters.

The prickly pear cactus is found in the south western states. Years ago it was taken to Australia, where it became a weed. It spread everywhere, because there was nothing in Australia that would eat it. A tiny moth was brought in from America to eat it. This soon reduced the number of prickly pear plants.

There are many more interesting facts to learn about insects. New insects are being discovered every day.

Glossary

abdomen: the back part of an insect's body. The abdomen is made up of six or more jointed parts.
antenna: a feeler on the top of an insect's head. Each insect has two antennae.
aphid: a small insect that sucks the juices out of plants. Aphids can cause a lot of damage to crops.
arthropod: animals which have bodies and legs made of jointed parts. Insects, spiders, crabs, and centipedes are all arthropods.
biological control: the way that animals are used by humans to keep down the numbers of an insect pest or plant. The animals eat the pests.
caddis fly: a type of insect that looks like a moth. Caddis flies have long legs and long antennae. They often fly at dusk.
camouflage: the shape of an animal's body or the color patterns on it which help the animal to hide in its surroundings.
carbon dioxide: a gas found in the air. All animals breathe out carbon dioxide.
caterpillar: the second stage in the life of a butterfly or moth. Caterpillars do not have wings.
cell: a very small part, or unit. Beehives are made up of hundreds of cells.
chamber: part of an insect's nest which is like a very small room. Chambers are used to store food and to nurse the young.
chitin: a strong material which makes the outside of insect skeletons hard.
cocoon: the silken case which protects the pupa of a moth.
cold-blooded: describes animals which cannot make their own heat. Their bodies are cold if the weather is cold and hot if the weather is hot.
compound eye: the large eye of an insect which is made up of many parts. Most adult insects have two compound eyes.
digest: to break down food inside the stomach and then pass it into the body.
drone: a male bee. Drones do not collect honey or pollen like the worker bees.
dung: waste matter that is passed out of the body.
excreted: passed out of the body.
exoskeleton: the hard "skin" of arthropods.
extinct: animals which are no longer living or found on earth.
file: a hard, rough vein on the wing of a cricket. The file is scraped over the other wing to make a sound.
flash color: a color pattern which is normally hidden under the wings. An insect suddenly shows this color to frighten an enemy.
foam: a mixture of soil and a liquid secreted by a female grasshopper.
focus: to be able to see something very clearly.
fossil: the remains of an animal or plant which is usually found in rocks.
gill: part of an animal used to breathe under water. Insect gills are often feathery.
habit: the usual way in which an animal lives.
haltere: the part of a fly that is shaped like a drumstick. The haltere is used to help the insect to fly straight. It is where the back wing used to be.
hibernate: to "sleep" or stay still through the cold winter. Some insects in hot countries sleep through the dry summers.
honeycomb: a layer of wax cells with five sides in which honey bees store their honey.
hopper: a young locust.
hoverfly: a type of fly that stays in one place in the air. Hoverflies look like wasps, but they do not sting.
insecticide: a chemical used to kill insects.
larva: the second stage of an insect. The larva hatches out of an egg.
lens: the clear, glassy part of an eye through which an animal sees.
Lepidoptera: the insect group which includes butterflies and moths.
life cycle: the changes in the life of insects (and other animals) from egg to adult.
lung: part of an animal used for breathing air.
maggot: a young fly. Maggots have no legs and move by wriggling.
malaria: a disease caused by a very simple, tiny animal. These animals live in the blood of other animals, and they can cause death.
mandible: the jaw or sharp, hard part of an insect's mouthparts. Most insects have two mandibles. Each can be long and curved.
midge: a very small fly. It sucks blood like a mosquito.
migration: the movement of animals from one area to another. These long-distance journeys happen at certain times each year.
mimic: to look like some other creature or object. Some insects mimic others that bite or are poisonous.

molting: changing an old skin for a new, larger one. All young insects grow by molting.

nectar: the sweet, sugary liquid that plants produce in their flowers. Many insects visit flowers to feed on nectar.

nerve: a tiny "cable" that carries messages from one part of an animal to another. Most nerves run to the brain.

nymph: the larva of an insect. Many nymphs look like tiny copies of their parents, but they have no wings.

order: one of the groups into which insects are split. Beetles belong to one order; flies belong to another.

oxygen: a gas found in the air. Oxygen is very important to all plants and animals. It is used in breathing.

pest: an animal or plant which eats something grown, built, or belonging to humans.

pollen: the tiny grains, sometimes called "dust," that are found in flowers.

pollination: the way in which pollen is moved from one flower to another to help make seeds. Insects are the most common carriers of pollen.

pulp: a squashed mixture of wood, or plants, and water. Pulp is used by some insects to build with.

pupa: a last stage in the life of some young insects. The pupa is the resting stage when the adult can take shape.

resistant: to become used to something. Insects that become resistant are no longer killed by poisons.

saliva: a liquid used in the mouth of an animal. Saliva helps to soften food.

sap: the watery liquid inside plants or leaves. This contains lots of sugar and other foods.

scale: a very small, thin plate found on the wings of butterflies and moths. Thousands of scales cover each wing.

secrete: to make and give off a liquid or juice. The stomach secretes juices which digest food.

segment: one of the jointed parts that make up an insect. The bodies, legs, and antennae of all insects are divided into segments.

skeleton: the hard parts of an animal which give its body some shape. Insects have their skeleton outside the body. Other animals have a bony skeleton inside the body.

social bee: a bee which lives in a nest with other bees. Some social bees, such as the honey bee, share the jobs within the nest.

species: a group of animals or plants which look alike and can breed with one another. It takes two adults of the same species to produce young.

spiracle: one of the tiny breathing holes on the outside of an insect's body. Spiracles are joined to tiny tubes inside the insect's body.

stage: a part of the life cycle of an insect. There are either three or four stages.

swarm: a large group of bees, ants, or wasps. They gather together to move to a new nest or to find mates.

termite: a type of insect that lives in large groups. Most termites live undeground or inside wood in the hot parts of the world.

thorax: the middle part of an insect's body. The wings and legs are attached to the thorax. It contains all the muscles that move the wings and the legs.

ultraviolet: a "color" of light which we cannot see. Insects see it as a type of pale blue.

vein: a long, thin tube which makes up the frame of an insect's wing. Each insect has a different pattern of veins in its wings.

warm-blooded: describes animals which can keep their bodies at a steady temperature. They do so by making their own heat. They can lose heat if they get too hot.

worker: a special type of female ant or bee that does not lay eggs. Most of the ants or bees we see are workers.

worker ant: a type of female ant without wings. Workers do not produce young.

Index

abdomen 6, 8, 13, 32
amber 9
ant 9, 24, 25, 38, 45
antenna 17, 28, 30, 32
ant lion 22
ant's nest 25
aphid 32, 34, 43, 45
arthropod 6
assassin bug 34

bedbug 34
bee 5, 24, 26, 27, 33
beehive 10, 26, 44
beeswax 45
beetle 10, 34, 35, 37, 41, 44
biological control 43
blood-sucker 19
book lice 41
buffalo gnat 33
bug 19, 34
bumblebee 24
butterfly 10, 14, 21, 28, 29, 32, 39, 44

butterfly larva 21
cabbage butterfly 43
cactus, prickly pear 45
carbon dioxide 18
caterpillar 20, 21, 24, 26, 29, 43, 45
chitin 12
cicada 34
clothes moth 40
cocoon 45
Colorado beetle 35
compound eye 16
cricket 15, 19, 30, 31

damselfly 36
DDT 42
diving beetle 37
Dobsonfly 37

dragonfly 8, 32, 37
drone 27
dung beetle 35

exoskeleton 6, 12, 14
eye spots 29

file 31
first insects 8
flea 15
flash color 29
fly 32, 33, 44
fossil 8, 9

glow worm 39
goliath beetle 34
grasshopper 20, 21, 30, 31, 45
ground beetle 34
grub 20, 45

haltere 32
honeybee 24, 44, 45
honeycomb 24
hopper 31
horsefly 33
housefly 23
hoverfly 32

insect
 breathing 18
 camouflage 23, 37
 eggs 20, 21, 23, 25, 26
 feeding 19
 feeling 17
 flight 14
 groups 10
 hairs 13, 17
 hibernation 7
 homes 23, 24
 movement 14, 15
 pests 11, 23, 35, 43, 45
 sight 16

skeleton 6, 12
skills 5
smell 13, 17
taste 13, 17
insecticide 42, 43

katydid 31

ladybug 45
lantern fly 39
larva 16, 20, 23, 34, 35, 36, 37, 43
 ant 25
 ant lion 22
 bee 26
 butterfly 21
 caddis fly 24, 36
 damselfly 36
 dragonfly 37
 dung beetle 35
 fly 32
 glow worm 39
 hoverfly 32
 ladybug 45
 mayfly 36
 midge 23, 32
 mosquito 32, 36
 spittlebug 34
 tiger beetle 34
 wasp 26, 27
leaf insect 38
leaf miner 22
Lepidoptera 10
life cycle 20, 21, 32
locust 30, 31, 43, 45
longhorn beetle 35

maggot 32
malaria 33, 43
mandible 19, 37
mayfly 36
midge 4, 23, 32
migration 14
mimic butterfly 29
mole cricket 30
mosquito 11, 13, 32, 33, 43
moth 10, 11, 19, 28, 29, 39, 44, 45
molting 12

nectar 26, 32, 44, 45
nymph 20, 21, 34, 37

oxygen 18

peppered moth 11
pollen 26, 44, 45
pollination 44
prickly pear cactus 45
pulp 24
pupa 20, 21, 45

queen ant 25
queen bee 26, 27
queen wasp 27

roach 11, 19, 40

segment 13
silk 5, 24, 45
silkworm moth 45
silverfish 40
sleeping sickness 43
social bee 26
spider 6
spiracle 18
spittlebug 34
stag beetle 10, 35
stick insect 38
swarm 27, 31
swimming insects 36

termite 5, 24, 45
 food gatherer 5
 nest 24
 nurse 5
 queen 5
 soldier 5
thorax 6, 8, 13, 32
tiger beetle 34
tree hopper 39
tsetse fly 43

ultraviolet 16

wasp 24, 26, 27, 33
wasps' nest 27
water boatman 36, 37
water scorpion 37
water strider 36
weevil 35
wing scale 28
woodlouse 6
worker ant 25
worker bee 26, 27

48